LAST DAYS

Last Days

TAMIKO BEYER

Alice James Books
FARMINGTON, MAINE
alicejamesbooks.org

10 9 8 7 6 5 4 3 2 1

Alice James Books are published by Alice James Poetry Cooperative, Inc., an affiliate of the
University of Maine at Farmington.

Alice James Books
114 Prescott Street
Farmington, ME 04938
www.alicejamesbooks.org

Library of Congress Cataloging-in-Publication Data

Names: Beyer, Tamiko, author.
Title: Last days / Tamiko Beyer.
Description: Farmington, ME : Alice James Books, [2021]
Identifiers: LCCN 2020045542 (print) | LCCN 2020045543 (ebook) | ISBN
    9781948579162 (trade paperback) | ISBN 9781948579407 (epub)
Subjects: LCGFT: Poetry.
Classification: LCC PS3602.E936 L37 2021 (print) | LCC PS3602.E936
    (ebook) | DDC 811/.6–dc23
LC record available at https://lccn.loc.gov/2020045542
LC ebook record available at https://lccn.loc.gov/2020045543

Alice James Books gratefully acknowledges support from individual donors, private foundations, the
University of Maine at Farmington, the National Endowment for the Arts, the Amazon Literary
Partnership, and the Maine Arts Commission, an independent state agency supported by the
National Endowment for the Arts.

Cover features a mural "A Daughter Migrates To The Mother Earth" by Jess X. Snow for Mural Arts
in Philadelphia in 2017 | Photo by Steve Weinik
Interior art by Mallinka1 / Shutterstock.

CONTENTS

🌿🌿🌿

🌿🌿🌿🌿

Dedicated to all the organizers, strategists, activists, artists, and healers imagining, building, and mapping the way toward a different future for us all.

"I have always known I learn my most lasting lessons about difference by closely attending the ways in which the differences inside me lie down together."
—AUDRE LORDE

"We need a vision that recognizes that we are at one of the great turning points in human history when the survival of our planet and the restoration of our humanity require a great sea change in our ecological, economic, political, and spiritual values."
—GRACE LEE BOGGS

"Some of us are surviving, following, flocking—but some of us are trying to imagine where we are going as we fly. That is radical imagination."
—ADRIENNE MAREE BROWN

WHAT IT MEANS TO BE HUMAN

Remember when we were very young,
we could disappear
and then reappear in the next room?

Our animal muscles have galloped
along in spite of our flawed sense of time.
I am the magic of a raised fist.

We break so easily: rib, shoulder,
psyche. Suddenly,
or over the drag of decades.

Then a beloved lights a match.
A stranger brings a glass of water.
One by one we touch our fingers to our wings.

And then the steady thrum—

TANKAS FOR WHAT COMES TOGETHER

At dawn, the great blue
heron curves the river, preens.
Stills as we approach.
In the narrative of our walk,
what comes together is a feeling:

we are the people,
the dogs, the birds. We emerge
from sleep singular—
then find each other. And that
is the best way of waking.

ESTUARY

Mixed-race woman walked
to the tidal river.

Torn leaves, plastic forks, empties
marked the queer slip

of boundaries. The leavings
of last night's high

tide. A warbler flitted
from branch

to branch in the bush
beside me, sung a complex

and familiar tune,
a trilled assertion of her tiny self—

I am, I am, I am.
Sing it, I said.

The cop drove slowly
through the empty

parking lot, brake lights flickering.
I took a breath. Not

safe. And not unsafe. A flash
of white down the river's bend: bald

eagle shifting in a tree. I took
off my shoes and stepped

onto the rocks
slippery with algae.

Every person has a name.
From lineage or paper.
Every creature breathes

until they don't,
breath wrenched by force
of bullet, flame, chain—

or breath released
in an easy exhale into night.
None of us know which way

we will go. But the odds
stack up by species,
neighborhood, race, and wealth.

We are, we are, we are:
Another warbler responds
from somewhere else.

A simultaneous translation
turns power
inside out: air into song,

fresh water into salt, bone
into stone. Our bodies as much
bacteria as self, our porous borders open—

the warbler, the algae, the rock.
We breathe out, and for now,
we all breathe in.

SOLSTICE

Once toxic waterway, now elegant,
iced at the edges. If the river were dredged,
we'd unsettle decades of chemicals

mucked under the mud. Someone with power
chose to leave what's quiet,
quiet. But when too many people have been torn

through, we gather at last. We call
into the blunt wind and the tin hiss
echoes back our slung-strung words.

Elsewhere, inside, someone is pouring
amber bourbon over a perfect sphere
of ice. He thinks the world blinks

on for him: open, open, open.
He polishes his keys and the bone
saw is an aching in his fingers.

Along the bank, the trees planted when white
men drafted a constitution are showing
their roots: gnarls pushing out of the packed dirt.

Like this, things come together
and then break apart. We grip in our fists
the ghost lights of some future.

Might be ours. The ice cracks.
Water surges, seeps. In the pause between,
the *we* of our bodies expands.

WE ARE BODIES IN BODIES WE ARE STARS

We are shining in the streets and in our homes, our bodies on fire in grief and rage.

We are seeds bursting open in fire.

We are soaked through to the bone in grief, breathing in grief with every gulp of air.

We are soaked through to the bone in rage, breathing in rage with every gulp of air.

We move toward each other, hands out and some distance away. We search for how to collapse the distance. We collapse the distance, some of us.

Some of us are fighting to remember the ancestral knowledge we carry in our bodies, all of us. The knowledge of how deeply we are connected to every creature, all of us.

Some of us don't need to learn this anew, some of us learned this from our grandmothers and ancestors who held onto wisdom when white people tried to rip it out and still they kept this knowledge like breathing. Some of us breathe this connection in every breath and with every step.

We are returning to the ocean and the forests, our bodies like waves, our bodies like seedlings. We are like mushrooms connected underground, like birds murmurating, all of us.

Because we are breathing, all of us.

We are breathing and our blood is running through our bodies, all of us.

Our breath travels out of our body and what was in us reaches someone else's body. We have little control over this. We are all breathing and sharing our breath. We have become so aware of this.

And maybe this is the beginning of something. Maybe this is the beginning of learning how to love beyond the boundaries of our selves. Maybe this is the beginning of learning how to love beyond the boundaries of our communities.

Some of us know this already and are waiting for the rest of us to catch up. Some of us are eager to learn how to love this way. Some of us are terrified to love this way, how vulnerable it is, and so are violently resisting it. Some of us feel exhausted just thinking about it. Some of us are not thinking about it at all.

We are all of us doing all of this. We are all of us breathing, shining in the streets and in our homes, breathing and shining.

UNRAVEL ALL SYSTEMS GO

What trades on systems? Weather, languages, economies.

In this labyrinth where exit equals null, the air deadens in the complex ductwork
behind matte walls. The escalator ascends and descends, again ascends, again
descends, again.

Beyond the corporate hurdy-gurdy, floodwaters roar and fires rise. Each too-hot and
too-cold day becomes its own faint counter rhythm to the up-tempo ditty.

And if I leapt over the railing—would that, too, be called a *natural disaster*? How many
king's horses and how many king's men? Falling I

> dream a rain soaked city
> > in this long hot season
> > > the cracked-off branch dangles low

Dear man upholding some kind of power in your three-piece suit. In your vested
interest. If you put down your phone would your leaden chest flower? How many win-
wins turn your skin whiter than already white? See those vessels running through?
Rivers of industry, a frantic pumping of a heart that may already be lost to the coin
toss. The reckoning might sounds like your cardiac arrest. May you know

> the center belies
> > our slow death—bait beat—
> > > the waxen flow below

Take the statistics again: 60 percent of our bodies are water and water makes up
71 percent of our earth's surface. The current rise in our global temperature is one
degree Celsius. Much more and we're toast. Yes.

No. Not a joke. I take each statistic into my warm, wet mouth. I chew, I swallow. Inside my gut they become true north. My friend, take out the glittering map. Fire up our fight song. Follow the

> star stroke in a broke boat
> —a still blue flotilla—
> so many waves dance

On this too-hot day my skin weeps with heat. Each limb is a question, each organ a dare.

By now, I know what it feels like to have taken part in a lifetime of the planet's destruction. How will it feel to take part in a system of recovery, of remedy?

> sting us alert—
> path of sky
> tongue fast to bodies try

WINTERING

A four-legged creature crosses the frozen river—

its spine shows.

I'm blinded by so much white.

My anger roars the skinny creature.

A truck dirties the snow for the price of gas,

crystallizes grit in fractal patterns.

The neighbor's wrist makes a splintering sound on ice.

The banks rise and fall under the sky's bowl.

My wrist makes a splintering sound on ice

like crystallized grit in fractal patterns.

A dirty truck for the price of gas,

my anger roars: skinny creature

blinded by so much white.

Our spines show.

We cross the frozen river.

CALL IT

We steer the car straight.
Behind the day, stars shine steady

as lighthouse signals: *Stay away, stay away, stay*
away. Weather refuses linear

progression—ice caps drifting
from out of the blue to where the hell.

The hurricane's eye was a slo-mo
turn and now the sun's a bright

squint. The rich nestle in their linens.
The rest of us scratch out syllabic

posts, our rheumy screens laden
with desire. Maybe *we're* the aliens.

Invasive species burning up bones
of our interplanetary ancestors.

What lousy shipwrecked guests.
And now, is a graceful exit even possible?

An easy slip off the highway
before the pileup, another grisly crash?

The car stalls. We look under
the hood, read the oil stains.

They say not for long, humans. Not long
for this breakneck break speed world.

COVID-19 TRIPTYCH

One

I spray 91-percent alcohol
across the kitchen counter
and remember

a chemist at Standard Oil first
discovered isopropyl alcohol.
Petroleum by-product, killer of virus.

The crust of the earth
shakes less now, a month
into quiet. Less stabbing,

less driving, less extraction.
I put my hand on the cold
earth. Feel how it exhales.

Two

My pantry stuffed
with bags of rice.
I gave in to the ancestral instinct

to gather the polished
grains close to my body. But
here, let me cook for you.

I am deliberate with fire,
generous with salt. I sing
into the gills of mushrooms.

Three

Teeth clank words
into place. A lock.
We are dying

and growing. All of us.
Virus, racism, fear.
What more to be incubated?

My body hot and messy, all
creatures, all the functions
of lung, gut, liver. My vast

landscape a system of sweep
and inoculation. The world outside
waits. Each fingernail makes

a solid house. Each eyelash
an earthquake,
each skin cell a spaceship.

TANKAS FOR WHAT COMES TOGETHER

At the seashore, wind
almost lifts our spindrift bodies,
sand scrapes our skin.
Let that sleek seal beat back the waves—
thunder amasses in cloud.

I do not believe
in the failure of caring
for each other. How
can I when the cascading wave
gathers us all in its rise?

EQUINOX

The girl stands on the edge of the only country she has ever known: blue-tiled roofs, the train-track heartbeat. The girl boards a jet plane and when she lands, the wide streets of the new country wash upon her like waves, depositing flotsam at her feet: broken color tv, paper crown, pacifier. Her name bleeds into the other alphabet. At exactly the midpoint, she dissolves.

Dear ghost girl, tell me
again the stroke order. I used to
know your form by heart.

Small figure tucked in a cul-de-sac driveway, 30 years later I lose our syllables, our age, race, and gender. We are in the back seat of a station wagon, we are crossing the avenues, we are walking at the base of skyscrapers. We make sounds with our mouths, we smell the burning brakes of subway cars, we lean into the sun. Our arms and legs swing, perpendicular pendulums, time- and space-keepers.

Sun on a fulcrum,
the light changes direction.
Say your only name.

Woman at the edge of a country she has only started to learn. I look down at thin cracks in the concrete and the seedings breaking through. I bend my knees, place my hands next to the green shoots. This: my arms and legs, my mixed race, my crackling heart. This: the dirt and glitter of my gender. This, the language I am stitched into.

ANCHOR IN THE MUD

One

They've gone with remediation.
Little bits of change
to refuse real forward. We need strategies

beyond bamboo strips: the enemy
is us, strange warriors
fighting our own bodies' survival.

The sky breaks. I put on a coat
that burns like sun reflecting off steel.
After months of barely cold, I am comforted

we have come to winter, puff and wool,
burning dust, paint layers. Seasons'
pace now unpredictable, the blue something

electric. We hold our collective
breath long enough to become transparent
on this city built on landfill. We quiver

above a sea happy to take
us back into its arms.
Animal into element.

Two

We shut off the lights, fill the refrigerator
with jars of water. The shoreline that hosted
the eagle this year finally iced over.

The most brittle bushes crushed
under the snow's weight: twigs encased
in gleaming ice like museum pieces.

If spring comes, we will take bets on what
sprouts again. Green becomes unimaginable
except in the deepest sleep.

Three

Boots and heels both
mine, all sorts of ways to go down.
Come up sweating. Blood and bones poised

to fight, queer defiance. These systems—
our relentless bodies processing
language, food, gesture. Come up

spitting. Defend, attack.
Do not leave money on the table,
solutions to those who hold power, your gender

to others. I keep my ugly
on, my girl close,
I keep the charge full.

CORRECT PRONUNCIATION

Citizens of now, show your papers.
Proof of employment, home address, full name.
The raised seal textured under your fingertips:
bristled pass into *America.*

Proof of employment, home address, full name:
terror roars as a white hand at the ballot box
slits our pass into American complacency.
This reckoning a bruised peach, soft spot turning

terror. A white hand at the ballot box,
a trick. It will take the rest of our lives,
this reckoning. Eat the peach, cut the soft spot out,
take your power back—

a trick that will take the rest of our lives.
Scale walls of metal and cement
taking your power back.
We gather like water, waves

slapping walls of metal and cement,
no edges but constant motion.
We gather like water. Waves
wearing away stone

edges with constant motion,
the work of undoing,
wearing away stone,
making space for our names.

The work of undoing
all the ways we've been mispronounced,
our full names taking up space
so that *citizen* flames like paper.

GENERATIONS

Issei

Plant-a-stone
generation. Have-faith-even-
the-sandiest-soil-
will-bloom-something generation.

そうね, 今
only cactus. But even:
cut away spike. Slice.
Water to quench our raging.

Body made for long
day, hard work. 仕方が
ない. If a barrack
we are living, we must bend

our minds to a pot full of rice,
river full of flashing fish.

Nissei

What happened to our
tongue, generation? The-nail-
that-sticks-up-gets-pounded-down

generation. We
go when army says go.
Take only what we carry.

Shame, the heaviest
suitcase. To lift our feet, tack
shame up between door-

ways, lacquer over
eyes, feed shame with cream of wheat
to the babies. Then, paste

silence over rage.

Sansei

Power-to-the-people
generation. Yellow-peril

supports-Black-power
generation. Why-aren't-we-

talking-about-this
generation. Harvesting

the hard knots: radish
or rage, no matter, dirt still

clings to the roots. We
yell into shame, raise our fists.

We build monuments
in the desert, rescue scraps

of culture, shake out
creases from musty kimono.

Later some open
our fists, wanting-more generation.

Yonsei

When the floodwaters receded, there we were, you-get-what-you-asked-for generation,
trying to find the pieces as best we could. But everything was slightly askew. Roofs
settling into odd angles, bicycle tires on hatchback rims, cherries smelling like oranges.
Even our faces didn't match. One brown eye, one black. Hands too big, tongues looping
out of our split mouths. We named it beautiful, this broken world we inherited.

And we hammered each
piece somewhere new, sowing
a field full of nails.

WHAT THE GRANDMOTHERS SAY

we broke bottles   electrified the abandoned
macadam with our rag-bone labor

smudgy fireflies in the humid night gathering a hundredfold
now   you limn the apple seeds

spit polish your steeled tongue
you gnaw   gnaw down your scattered hunger, child,

bank in lusty angles
while your hatchlings in their clotted nests uncoil   wet from shell
        beak a widening raw

all our rage unslaked—

LAST DAYS

One

>   *safe is an interpretation* —Kate Greenstreet

We didn't expect the eagerness that filled us on the last days of empire. For what, we couldn't exactly say.

Metal glistened on the streets in the hot September days. The sun no longer a dandelion; the sun most definitely a muzzle. When it set, the Corporation—keen to kill the dark—flipped the switch.

Then, the marble facades of buildings were suddenly up-lit, streetlights swirled incandescent, and thousands of people hurtled through the furnace of synthesized laughter, pop songs, and an unlimited desire for all.

///

Some of us were on the edges, blocking out the canned sounds and lights as best we could. Building something new, something old. We could feel the northern half of our planet begin to tilt away from the sun.

I am on the cusp of change, and the curve is shifting fast.

It was an experience and then it was a memory. And then a system of belief, a way to navigate the dissolving world.

I wanted to become more salt wind, less reflection. To become quiet enough to hear the ancestors.

ANCECSTORCHORUS:

Find the source at the underwater

roots, at the mudline:

fragile strands of a new language

among cattails and seed casings.

Trust the fibers

will lean in the right direction,

will not mislead you.

Child, we have always laid

one strand over, then under the next,

over and under, over and under—

until something like true

meaning emerges from the twist

of our fingers. This basket

                                                is for you: an exhortation, a map.

                                                Soon you will need to reach

                                                all of us in this river of time

                                                with the truest sentences

                                                you can weave.

There were five of us in that small apartment, hauling water, coding and decoding, soldering metal, constructing strategies, drafting poems. I lifted heavy objects and learned to stitch up an open wound.

I no longer thought of myself as a girl. I was often afraid. At the same time, I glistened in the everyday fever brought on by Wave's eyes opening, the morning sky breaking.

When we met, Wave said holding on was dangerous. The taste of hope could make us reckless. I knew what she meant, but despite ourselves, I came to love how she tasted more than I loved any fruit on my tongue.

ANCESTORCHORUS:

                                                Light breaks the glass

                                                separating you

                                                from the present.

                                                The dangerous words

> chime in the wind, spike
> into sand and grass.

> Behold the other kind of blade:

> power of seed

> turned blossom, turned fruit.

In the afternoons we would cross the river on the train, skimming ancient tracks into the center of the city where things were bought and sold on a grand scale. We slid into the gaps of commerce, knowing *all warfare is based on deception.*

So many people were building scaffolding against crumbling structures, using incantations from their fathers as mortar.

But some attempted to excavate the signals buried deep within their bodies; some tried to listen to their heartbeats.

Those were the ones we were looking for. We slipped them a scrap of paper, then dissolved back into the crowd.

ANCESTORCHORUS:

> Words can obscure like clouds
> or reveal like the tidal pull.
> Do you remember rain?

> *The state of emergency is also always*
> *the state of emergence.* Where does the water go
> when ocean draws out its lowest tide?

When the new recruits followed the poem to find us, we put them to work or gave them maps to others in need of their skills. We were hundreds of loose groups across the country, fashioning transformation out of starlight and strategy, spindrift and solidarity.

///

I was impatient for the waking, the sharp sensation of light and promise. I thought I understood.

But there was still so much to learn. Wave reminded me of the libraries they had shut down years ago, their floors like silk, books heavy with promise. That's where we went: picking the locks, scraping away the dust, memorizing what we could.

Power grids, water-sewer lines, and fiber-optic cables snaked their way across the city. We became deft in mapping and coordinates, diversion and distraction. We discovered the patterns the Corporation relied on, found the back doors, planted the traps with care.

Creating new economies in the heart of capital required cunning and poetic imagination. We knew we were being watched when the NICE drones paused above our fire escape.

But cooking and dancing were not yet crimes. We could plan just as well stirring the pot in three-four time as in stillness around the kitchen table.

Patience is in the living. Time opens out to you. We hummed and we sang. We simmered soup and kneaded flour and water. We mapped out the next tactics.

Two

The body, with its arms up, is a kind of miracle —Aracelis Girmay

We knew it would change and it did. Mostly we were prepared for it, but the cold policing still struck us hard.

We got the warning just in time from Roe down at the bodega. The cops were sawing at the heavy chains across the door downstairs.

I strapped the typewriter to my back, and Wave gathered up her colored notebooks as the cops' boots thundered up the stairwell.

The kitchen window jammed.

Wave heaved her shoulder under the sash and it budged a few more inches. Terra and May slid out, scaled down the fire escape. Wave followed, but when I tried the typewriter got wedged, and I couldn't move.

The Corporate police battered their rifle butts at the door we had reinforced with steel months ago. Wave put her arms around my ribs and pulled. I toppled out, our arms tight around each other.

We shimmied down the rope and traveled fast, out of the city's most rumbling sections.

Terra and May went south, across the harbor. Roe stayed to break the code. Wave and I ran tight together, broadcasting alarm signals over encrypted channels.

We spoke the words, leaning into dangerous conversations. We knew there was at least one spy among us, but we had to take the risk.

ANCESTORCHORUS:

                      Say a name

                                 and see its familiar

                                              float by.

The present was a sheet of glass suspended in midair.

We loosened our fists, wiped down the sweat, then gripped again. We became intimately familiar with our weapons and the soles of our feet, with *ghost as a verb*.

We walked north, mostly on frontage roads. Even though we had been preparing all this time, we had thought somehow it might turn out differently.

But we were queers and people of color—we grew up learning how to read the signs on white people's faces, on the hands of cops, and in the sound of breaking glass.

We knew it was long past time.

ANCESTORCHORUS:

                                       And then the fall, the syntax-strange days.

                                           Translate tree roots, terror.

                                              The code will be full

of false starts, trapdoors, dead

ends. Where your shadow

rises, keep your ear to the sky. Make

meaning from the ground up. The only

way to pray.

Three

Words work as a release—well oiled doors opening and closing between intention, gesture. ... words encoding the bodies they cover. —Claudia Rankine

Turns out the Corporate code was less verb than adjective. I should have known. I should have anticipated it would show us only the glittering decorations and never the bones.

The instructions felt funny in my mouth, and I could feel deep in my gut that they weren't quite right. But Roe, still in the city, insisted they were solid.

I tried opening my mouth again but couldn't summon anything. Wave looked at me for a long time, patient like the ever-repeating ocean we were headed toward.

Who was I to contradict Roe, who had been in this for so much longer than me? Since Occupy, at least, he always said.

"Listen, I think..." I started, just as we heard the dull whine of a drone.

Wave grabbed my hand and we ran low to the ground into a building that was part iron, part rust, part decomposing vegetative matter.

The explosions disoriented me from the horizon. I thought about how the sound of the letter "l" mimics the fold between sky and earth, how that was easier to distinguish than where water meets the sky, the lapping "w."

"There's another meaning underneath," I said to Wave as the ancient windows shattered and we covered our heads with our arms. I wanted five minutes with the typewriter and code, but there was no time. We heard three more drones arriving.

Wave located a storm drain. We pried the cover off with a piece of rebar.

Then it was all dark and stink, slime and shadow for miles.

ANCESTORCHORUS:

> Blades, cusp of a season.

> Wet territories wax and wane with strategy.

> Incipient boundaries:

> south node, the open door.

> See anger turn stride.

> See stride turn tide.

> Because it is not the horizon you are fighting for, child.

> No—

> the whole damn sea and sky.

Possibly Roe was a spy. We never found out. When we emerged from the subterranean labyrinth after midnight, we found a town shut tight, asleep but bristling with Corporate flags.

Our signal gone, no code, no text from Roe or anyone.

Even with the stink of sewer clinging to me, I smelled it. The salt in the air. And then the rhythmic crashing—ocean's exhale. "Listen," I whispered, this time without falter.

"I hear it," Wave whispered back, grinning.

"I made a mistake," I said. "We shouldn't have followed Roe's instructions, and I knew it three days ago. I knew it but couldn't say it."

Wave nodded. "It's hard to trust the body."

///

We reached the beach in silence. The rolling waves, the wind, the night, our two tiny bodies at the edge of the vast sea.

We waded into the cold shock, and then Wave dove, headfirst into her rising namesake. Her hair streaming behind her, her arms arcing in the night.

Where our power resides was never a conceptual question. I understood that now, shivering under the piercings of light in the night sky.

Wading out of the ocean, Wave said, "The only time I was truly trapped was in that other city—landlocked, no sea wind, no grace."

I nodded. "Let's dance." And we did, holding each other tight, our bodies flaring.

Four

I am a scar, a report from the frontlines, a talisman, a resurrection. —Audre Lorde

We buried our ruined clothes at the foot of the sea cliffs, changed into dry ones. In the growing light we gathered seaweed scalloped along the tide line. We made a driftwood fire and ate. The sea lettuce was all ocean and chlorophyll on my tongue, salty green between my molars. My saliva was the light reflecting off the waves.

I held my palms over the dancing flames and then held my tin cup to the sky. It became a wine glass, and the wine was a silver lake where tiny fish darted in the shadows: our friends swimming naked.

ANCESTORCHORUS:

Dawn. The way the day comes

into focus. The sun a sudden

happening on the horizon:

thinnest edge of light

flooding into abundant sphere.

Gulls fly into the magenta hallelujah,

elegant sentences of grace.

Shake the sand from your hair, child.

Live the hunger edge down.

Open your mouth when it rains.

We began walking north again. There were others, somewhere in the dunes, living in shelters erected decades ago for artists and writers and then forgotten. They were unraveling language and building what comes next.

One foot after the other, the sand packed and wet beneath us as the tide drew itself out. The heavy typewriter strapped to my shoulders "It could be another trap," I said.

Wave turned to look at me, her wild hair decked in sunlight and wind. "Yes. It could."

We kept walking.

The shoreline rasped, the liminal space between earth and water. That was power—articulating the transition in my body. And maybe that was love—my heart opening wider to Wave and the pain of the world when we breathed in, when we all breathed in, knowing that there we were: in tender battle with the deepest waves within us.

Epilogue

When we finally found May and Terra again it was in another city by the sea. They arrived leading a formation of a hundred others, bikes veering into turns from all directions, hair blowing in the wind. I was translating the code and Wave shouted instructions, kicking up her boots and dancing.

And then the army descended, Corporate logos on their weapons flashing in the most vibrant digital red, white, and blue. We knew we needed to slip into the sea: mermaid, selkie, outlaw.

But we had one more code to dispatch, and we sent the warriors to the most lightly guarded section of the city, speakers rattling a false trail, May at the front, her biceps bulging, Terra at the rear.

I realized then that all of us in concert made up Sun Tzu's definition of a leader. Beyond the city's edge, the icy waves applauded with the ancestors: *Mudline and fibers, syntax and streetlights, fruit and rice to share.*

I knew what they were saying. The words we script together are mortar and bricks of the new world. They cannot be anything but.

TANKAS FOR WHAT COMES TOGETHER

Bones fill my tank, sharp
gas stink—eons
of nesting in earth.
I pump in geologic time:
dirt to oil to fire.

Forgive us our quick
flame, the end of patience,
our jet-fuel canyons.
Once microbes in the sun,
we've become the heated air.

EXPERIMENT IN REVOLUTION, 2016

Between structural change
and my planted body:
an exploded box.

Our arms linked
the whole way home. Fire
works. A new name then

to my mouth again.
Her mouth theirs.
Race the twisted rope.

Sandra Bland. Time a trigger.
Alton Sterling. Justice
throttled. Philando Castile.

So we're living
in each other's
hands. Impossible

to deadhead roses. *For all of us
this instant*. No law
sound to carry. Steady July

sun. Catch
the backbeat
home. Black bodies

blocking freeways, breaking
the starless night.
Showing up

with your salt
on my lips. Call
it like it is. Queer

and drenched
in color, in blood.
Our muscles

are spears.
Our voices sirens,
our torsos drums.

A large
experiment
in bodily

revolution. Joy,
come
get me.

SOLSTICE

I pick up a small stone, honeycombed, rust-
colored. Lighter than I expect, like driftwood
or ember. A bit of pumice in my palm.
Rocks don't lie. What gets buried deep

eventually touches fire. And with enough heat
even the hardest stone melts then rises to surface sky.
No fixed form on this earth. We are so much more
than our genetic code. How much pressure will we endure

before we burst out of our bodies, rain
down like burning rock? The longest day brings
the dark. When the ground rumbles
I turn my shoulders to the mountains.

Open my mouth. Eat
the midday sun.

BLUE PASSPORT

It slips me in the back door.

In the late 70s and early 80s, our ragtag family traveled every two years to the American Embassy in Tokyo. I collected visa stamps. I would never be a citizen, they told me, of the country where my baby teeth fell out and my adult teeth grew in. I never learned to bow in the right way at the right time. That was part of it. I kept the passport as evidence.

///

It is not a talisman. It gives limited protection. Evidence: Executive Order 9066.

The Roosevelt memorial quotes FDR, 1940: *We must scrupulously guard the civil rights and civil liberties of all our citizens, whatever their background.* I sit next to the larger-than-life statue of Fala, Roosevelt's Scottish Terrier, who he took everywhere. Fala's bronze ear tips are shiny from the strokes of a hundred thousand strangers carrying a rainbow of passports.

"He signed the evacuation order in 1942," I say. My mother nods. Silent, we gaze at the next sculpture: our mouths in relief.

///

I pass so easily
my heart flutters.

This is a medical condition.
Your bone marrow
does not match mine.

///

Passport with holes so my image
fragments into confetti-shaped shadows.
Passport smelling of milk and rice.

Passport guarantees _____ or nothing at all.
Passport my ticket to ride
the ferris wheel and watch

the beach town spread below, the sea
a thin, blue line
licking the sand. Tiny people hold

tiny sticks of cotton candy,

and a gull wheels by.
Passport sings along:
America, America.

///

Aliases I have known: pioneer girl in a cotton bonnet and a heart full of manifest
destiny. Never a laundry worker. Never a cook. Once, a cowboy in rawhide chaps,
riding into the desert sunset. Never a prisoner. No one said: "That's where camp was."
We didn't know what camp was back then.

///

Hold it like a meringue, like a piecrust flaking into three pm teatime.

Lock it in the safe; don't forget where you put the key.

Tie it around your neck with a string—a third, fluttery breast.

When they come for you, place it over your heart. It just might slow a bullet.

ROOT AND RISE

One

Full moon rising: *Fed and watered   human   what*
                           will you do   with those hands?
                                  all those wounds   open?

Two

I am descended
from immigrants
and internees
laborers and
settlers

Three

Full moon risen: *Find how you must grow*

Four

          Seeds break through   loose soil

                   at the U.S.   border

babies wrenched from their parents   by men whose paychecks   I   write

              laying in rows of cots I bought

Five

We were 12 in a barrack we were the nails pounded down anyway we were abandoned
in the winter desert where the wind was sand and the grey mountains immobile as the
sun rose over them and the moon set behind them and the wind blew grains of sand
into the corner of our mouths and the crevices of our teeth but brought no trace of the
ocean from where we came

Six

seeds root with light   a child wakes   two-thirty a.m. screaming

        in one prison   her mother in another   no mountains

           no flight

Seven

We were 50 in a barrack we were children under the eye of a bayonet we were starved
in moonlight and we made dresses from newspapers and we began to disintegrate we
began to burn and in the screaming a bird rose into the night sky to meet the moon
broad-winged and bloody

Eight

Pour me my arrow, moon

        String me my bow, cast your light on the strands

      that connect me to her to him to them   Illuminate the web each of us has woven   in love and in hate   with care and with indifference

in complicity and struggle   Let us find our way

EXPERIMENT IN REVOLUTION, 2020

Waterfalls of ones and zeros, waterfalls
of fractures. We are boxes
in screens and in the streets we scream.

We have been here too long,
washing our hands over and over and over again,
the floorboards wet with rain.

Mom's sign says *Defund and Demilitarize
the Police*, her schoolteacher
printing bold on poster board. She's all the way

on the other side of the country
where the police are a battering ram
echoing escalation, the same

as this side of the country, the same
in every part of the country, gripping guns
like power, long sticks swinging

from their hips. I see their violence again
as I scroll through the news,
waterfalls of ones and zeros

missing George Floyd's breathing
missing Breonna Taylor's heartbeat,
missing Tony McDade's dreams.

Mom goes alone to the protest
with her carefully printed sign,
and she asks me what did you make

for dinner, how are the dogs,
how do we become
patterns of stars, what

smoke do we etch across the sky,
when do we erupt,
and what does lava taste like... No,

that's me asking her these questions,
mother of the island, mother
of the saltwater sea:

How do we light ourselves up again,
after so many cycles of smoke and spark,
how do we let rage lava into birth?

21ST CENTURY FABLE

Catastrophe came at night. Missiles arcing in the starless sky. Masses of people hungering in hot, spiked cages. The mouth of an endless forest fire.

When she woke, she realized it was more daylight than dream. She turned this way and that, but there were no other views from any window—south facing or north.

///

Her privileges were fine sores all over her skin and organs.

What if I formed my mouth into questions?

She tossed her burning lipstick and opened her thin lips. She bent her right leg over her left, twisted her arms, leaned forward, looked up. She asked about her place on the grid, the pale squares around her.

///

Maybe order doesn't grow happiness.

So she stepped into a lightning storm.

The chance of being struck so small and so spectacular. Full tilt, she ran across wettest night. Already, she could smell the heady mix of electricity and flesh. But no strike came for her.

In the morning, she wrung out her dress and stripped off another layer of ideas.

She opened her mouth and tested out a new spell. She was wobbly, but people she knew were family began to arrive.

She ladled out oden she had kept warm on the stove.

///

The hands of the city's clock tracked the progress toward the towers of cash. Time skewed.

She slid a soup tureen across the floor at the ten-grand-a-plate fundraiser. She was lovely in her sashay. Security couldn't say how she got in. The power at City Hall went out.

She tried to gather up all the migrating songbirds on the sidewalk. Too many mistaking skyscraper for sky.

She raised her arms in sorrow and more family stepped into them.

///

She folded a paper crane. It became a sparrow perched on the stoplight, singing loudly into stillness. No machines. No cars.

Black women and femmes chanted incantations of their ancestors and the cages at Rikers blew open. San Quentin dissolved. Framingham shattered. All the prisons evaporated.

The people who had been outside traveled to meet the people who had been inside. The elders led with bowls of water, ripe peaches, and armfuls of peonies that soaked the air with sweetness. At the back, she carried blankets and pillows for those who needed a long rest in the field where bars had turned into calendula, orange petals reflecting back the sun.

///

She cut her lip because of the dryness in the air. Then came the tornados. All the pieces were there; she had to trust what was impossible and true.

Her family were people of lightning, cranes, and microbes. Too tough to quit. *We keep each other safe.*

SWEET BRANCH STITCHED TO BITTER TREE

After many sleight-of-hand
days the sun squares itself
on the wall. *Tart* is what my tongue
says against the slice I lay
across it. *Sweet* say my molars.

This apple grown from graft. Cut
open the myth starred in every core.
Seeds are just one way to abundance.
Come, love—we spin
and spin to our very own pleasure.

SUBTERRANEAN HAIBUNS

> Night's hours crawl across
> the floor's thin bones I fall into
> my mind's other.

There, the three-legged pig is not a pig but a pheasant. The bird is part of a Japanese folk story that taught me young boys will always have allies if they are good and strong and true. The problem with symbols: they are bundles of stone. I have so often been crushed by them.

The *why* behind the sacred. Some secrets are best kept secret. Once we open our mouths, toads or jewels spill out. Imagine carrying all that hardware in your stomach. Months of due diligence, kicked in your belly. And it's not even a baby; it's a stone.

When I was born, the cicadas chirped to themselves, a desperate situation. There were not many others in the room. My mother and father and a person to help bring me into the world.

I as *I* was not planned for, despite their desire to create a being.

> Take a walk with you
> along the rusting shoreline.
> The moon's bare candor.

Systems say go. It's not sleep I'm looking for, it's a complete surrender. The cicadas rasp as loud as engines and the clock on the wall is a second-by-second demonstration of how time moves.

So much of our today shaped by *god* and *conquest*. But what has happened for
millennia will continue to happen. Because of wind. Because of sun. Because of
dirt and because of water. Because we come at the problem from one way and then
another. Quinoa, mantra, ninja. Colonizers take, take over, and hold on.

Until we make our victory out of thin air and organizing.

It was hot; my body incubated. We keep arriving with new yeses at the ocean's shore.
The physicality of the sea, how it sucks from below, crashes against the sky, gives us
back our stripped bones. You can go out closed and then come back with your heart
wide open. Both diamonds and frogs, what I no longer need to hold.

I throw a pebble clear across the day to land in your lap. Today it was your fingers I
was noticing. How long they are, rimmed by tiny white moons.

Mid-sky—stone blazing
across light years, unquenched.
We step into the sun.

The cicadas are singing their summer swan song. The pulsing light sparking the trees
of June is gone, already burrowed into roots, leaves now dark and dusty. The year curls
into itself. And we are here, on a precipice.

I give you an anaphora, a talisman. When I said symbols are burdens, I did not mean
it. In this firestorm of astonishing speed, a stone is something solid to hold on to.

So I say everything will be fine, and what do we do but say yes—because the cicadas
are going full throttle ahead, and what the insects know, if they know anything at all,
is the sheer force of life and the primacy of song. I have come with pen and paper

to record the journey of two beings, or the light that stands for two beings because sometimes we have only trace evidence of the sun after it has disappeared.

Love, the cicadas buzz into themselves. They will soon be silent and translucent, leaving us only the body's silent language.

Deep forest floor
muffles our footsteps. We search
the taproot, the source.

Too many times I have turned away from the magnificent trail of dirt and desire. Too many times I have searched for a subterranean lagoon, but couldn't get beyond the iron gate.

Your scarred neck. That's where my confessions lie. We come out swinging because wilderness always risks danger. This is a howling against fences and deception. A howl of funerals.

How many rituals have we lost? Giving up brings no reckoning and is never enough. There is only one foot and then the other. No underground shortcuts.

You said beautiful must be broken to remain beautiful, quoting a woman who herself broke in the end, unable to anchor. But she left us this: every morning breaking across mud and water.

Us unfolding our legs to come closer to the ground. You, gorgeous mosaic of fragments, loss, survival. Me, impossible to live in a body not set trembling like a cello string. So we do.

Attend the world's every move and come undone at every line.

OPEN

Your lip cracks, sweet
water. Like to like we bleed.

Our tidal current widens the way. Not
a breaking. An easing.

Uprivered by salt winds
to home horizon, our border

hearts open. Our reed bodies fill brimful
with river water, fill brimful with rain.

I VOW TO BE THE SMALL FLAME

My people, we have found
too shallow our roots
in this land full of boulders.

But when the satellites fall
I vow to use my good
sense of direction to find you.

Songs make provisions—
all the spells to turn our capillaries
into branches—

sea waving sky. I vow
a ravenous undoing.
I vow to love the fire always.

TANKAS FOR WHAT COMES TOGETHER

Catch the wild yeast,
see it devour flour
and water, rise up.
Soy sauce and miso take years
of resting in the dark. Sometimes

a constellation
is best seen out of the corner
of your eyes. Clarity
comes sideways. Try it head on
and watch it disappear.

[   ]

{The space}

between leaf
and virus.
Between rain

drop and heat:
the ground rising to meet another wash.

Between what we know
and what we do:

fueling the car, eminent
domain, new
phone, the compost
pile, a cache of seeds.

Between now
and what will unfurl.

[Two hummingbirds zoom just outside my line of vision. They dart
among the butterfly bushes, asters still blooming in the last days of
summer—September 20, 2019, with 408.50 parts per million of
atmospheric carbon in the air. Children flood the streets, demanding
a future.]

{What if the future}

Is behind us? (Not passed or past. Just out
of our sight line. Waiting to be sensed. Or just—
there. No expectations of being found or caught
up to or arrived at.)

Is rooted? The maple behind me,
leaves just starting to turn.

Is a memory just under the shoulder
blades of every person on Earth?

[Flight is an option, sometimes the only option, sometimes not an
option, sometimes a bad option. Flight is a form of travel, five
gallons of jet fuel per mile. Most birds have hollow bones. The ruby-
throated hummingbird's wings move in the shape of an eight. She
flies forward and backward, hovers, changes direction in an instant.]

{Can be seen}

in the rearview: more
cars, thin branches

etched, a hidden
trio of colors—

red, yellow, green shining
away from me.

Through the windshield: white
lines on pavement, more

cars, apartment buildings
with the curtains drawn down.

[In their migration they chase the dying flowers. Open, open, open,
closed. Stay still for just one. Wings opening and closing in the space
behind me like the monarch on a zinnia. Orange against orange
against blue. Time like light against the bodies defining passage. Sun
browning my skin outlines a feather.]

{Cannot be seen}

as I walk backwards, eyes
closed: the witchgrass
and its seed heads,
the hummingbirds chasing.
The sap running slow,
drawing down, the maple
turning toward winter.

Not behind me nor in my periphery:
a man decides,

the gates swing shut,
the locks click and click and click.

Closed. People in the streets
hoist signs, banners wave open.

{I am the sound of the wings unfurling from my scapula.}

[A spider's carcass blows across the page, tiny husk. Beneath the teak
cabinet other spiders thread their webs from baseboard to floorboard,
suck insects into husks. A hummingbird weaves its nest from spiders'
webs and stems. The future zooms just outside my line of vision,
chasing the past.]

{Yet to come}

structures that cast the longest

night into the shortest day.

Prescision in the placement

of stones in a circle.

We call it ancient but

what if it is future?

And if the future is behind us,

can we yet arrive?

[I carry my weight on my heels. I am always leaning forward. Both statements are true.]

{Is singing}

and swings
its flashlight, swings
its lamp. Light, dark,
light, dark, light, dark, dark.
The future
has something
to say. It writes itself
across our backs.

        [

                ]

THE FLOOD

In the theater of the former capitol, dancers and musicians swept bullets and rotten wood off the stage.

On the night of the performance, their costumes fluttered, rags in the updraft.

Rigged lights flickered like intermittent birdcalls, then steadied.

The audience breathed—as a single, taut animal.

At the curtain's rise, the hard knot in every one of our throats burst, caught fire, became a wail.

The dancers raised their arms in unison.

A slow procession of tears flowed from our eyes to chins to laps.

The drummers drummed.

Our tears pooled on the floor, lapped at our ankles.

Wind and string instruments winged through bullet holes and hunger.

When we all finally swallowed the last note, the theater was a salty lake.

Folding chairs became boats on which we floated into the night, our bodies strangely light: mirrors to the stars in the cloudless sky, wings unfurling on our backs.

EQUINOX

Dear child of the near future,
here is what I know—hawks

soar on the updraft and sparrows always
return to the seed source until they spot

the circling hawk. Then they disappear
for days and return, a full flock,

ready. I think we all have the power
to do what we must to survive.

One day, I hope to set a table, invite you
to draw up a chair. Greens steaming garlic.

Slices of bread, still warm. Honey flecked with wax,
and a pitcher of clear water. Sustenance for acts

of survival, for incantations
stirring across our tongues. Can we climb

out of this greedy mouth,
disappear, and then return in force?

My stars are tucked in my pocket,
ready for battle. If we flood

the streets with salt water, we can
flood the sky with wings.

GENESIS: FEATHERLING

One

The word untethers itself
from root, from soil—
floats on the first breeze.

Water was a mirror,
and then it was a lung. Marsh grass
swaying with every breath.

Two

Salt residue on my tongue. The moon
blooms and thins. The ancient cotton across my breast
shreds. Muscles lean, joints supple. God-
like. I know there are others—
hungry. In this marsh or the next
or the next. The redwing
blackbird trills. I do not see it.
I do not see it, but I hear it.
I hear it and know it is kin.

Three

First migration south.
Constellation-led, sun-bound.
Pray the sky our wings.

MURMURATION

I was born golden out of the belly-egg.
Microbes and parasites said,
Nice to meet you featherling.

Said, *Share and share again.*
And I did because it was the right
thing to do—and what else did I know?

Humans were never meant to fly, birds
were never meant to speak. Yet here
we are, wings skimming updrafts

warmed by ancient asphalt.
I catch a thermal and rise
and rise and rise. Under the sun's gaze

every muscle, every feather shaft shifts
awake. My blood-pulse trills
a steady boom-boom call to flock.

We meet midair, family
and strangers, a dark net turning
across the sky. Mystery of mutation

an exultation of human birds
wheeling above disintegrated cityscapes,
our voices blending into gathering song.

Dear planet, dear Earth, when we alight
we will thread the dirt

with our beaks, skim the water on our bellies,
land on new grass with tender feet.

We will come home, *generation, generation
regeneration*, singing

of blood and bone, keratin and filoplume, fin and gill, antennae and thorax,
bloom and stem, pistil and stamen, magma and lava, salt water, river water, waterfall.

BIRDS OF A FEATHER

A future zuihitsu

Our eyes bend what they cannot see. The end of deepest winter.

I suspect things are growing again. After sleeping soundly for centuries, muddy buds are pushing into the crunch of air.

Will we miss the deep freeze? The sound of snow falling on snow?

Many days I start off as you and end leagues away.

Is it my ambiguous skin? Not human, not amphibian, not fowl, not insect, but mammal.

And what of the cyber creatures?

Of the people, we say. A casing as bright as a beetle of yore. What it means to never be alone again.

Imagine the ancient scientists in their white coats standing forever with hands behind their backs. Heads bowed in prayer or punishment. Either way, we're their splayed creation myth—hubris or bridge.

A whole planet of things to restore or discard, swirling in currents, washing up into caves.

All day, I waited for the light to hit just so. Rib bones, aluminum, rebar. Waited for a sign—what to do with this inheritance.

Did we ask for such patience, such flight?

All day, I watched the flowers turn their new faces to the old sun. That's devotion. Or maybe instinct. Have we learned the difference?

The sex of flowers undoes me. Such delicate anatomy.

I want to be fingers not folded but crane. I want to be salt to your kingdom. I will be bird to your wire.

NOTES AND ACKNOWLEDGMENTS

"What It Means to Be Human"
With thanks to Aja Monet for the prompt.

"Solstice"
Dedicated to water warriors everywhere, across time.

"Unravel All Systems Go"
Dedicated to my Corporate Accountability comrades, for all the work you do challenging transnational corporations with endless love and determination.

"Generations"
With gratitude to Alexis Pauline Gumbs for this prompt, and for the beautiful writers of the M/otherlands seminar.

"Last Days"
Gratitude for the grace of these lines: "I am on the cusp of change, and the curve is shifting fast." - Audre Lorde, *A Burst of Light*; "All warfare is based on deception."—Sun Tzu, *The Art of War*; "...the state of emergency is also always the state of emergence."

—Homi Bhabha, 1986 forward to Frantz Fanon's *Black Skin, White Masks*; "Patience is in the living. Time opens out to you." —Claudia Rankine *Citizen*; "ghost as a verb" —Kate Greenstreet.

"Experiment in Revolution, 2016"
Dedicated to all the warriors, organizers, and activists in the movement for Black Lives. Thanks to Duriel E. Harris for inviting me to create an Experiment in Joy in July 2016, and to Patti Lynn, Michél Legendre, cori parrish, and Charlotte Beyer for taking part in this experiment with me. "For all of us / this instant" is by Audre Lorde from "A Litany for Survival" (*The Black Unicorn*).

"Root and Rise"
Dedicated to all migrants crossing borders seeking a full and beautiful life, and to the organizers, activists, and lawyers at the U.S. border and beyond fighting for the lives, rights, and dignity of migrants and immigrants. Thanks to Sarah Faith Gottesdiener for the *Many Moons* workbook.

"21st Century Fable"
Written with deep gratitude to all those engaged in abolition work. And much thanks to Tricia Hersey and the Nap Ministry for the wisdom that rest is resistance.

"Subterranean Haibuns"
Originally drafted at 3:15 am over the course of a summer, with thanks to Bernadette Mayer.

"I Vow to Be the Small Flame" and "Equinox (Dear child of the near future)"
So much gratitude and love to Sarah Gambito and fellow Kundiman participants in Writing Toward Radical Love and Light Your Lantern: virtual, collaborative writing space led by Sarah in 2016 and 2018 in response to the presidential election and the ensuing assault on the lives, rights, and dignity of people of color and immigrants.

"Murmuration"
Although I drafted this poem before I read adrienne maree brown's *Emergent Strategy*

and her beautiful ideas on flocking, the final version of this poem and the whole book owes a debt to brown's brilliant thinking and moving in love toward the future we can create together.

Many thanks to the editors and staff of the journals and anthologies in which some of these poems first appeared, often with different titles and in radically different forms: *Adrienne, Black Warrior Review, The Common, Contemporary Verse 2, Denver Quarterly, DIAGRAM, Discover Nikkei, DUSIE, Foglifter, The Fourth River, The Idaho Review, Opening Lines: the 2011 Girls Write Now Anthology, Hysteria, The Margins, Other Rooms Press, Paradise Now, Tupelo Quarterly*, and *The Volta*.

With gratitude to the Massachusett, Wampanoag, Pawtuket, and Nauset peoples, on whose lands I wrote this book. These lands and water, particularly the Neponset river, are the blood, bones, and breath of these poems.

Deep thanks and love to my family, friends, and co-conspirators. Enormous gratitude to cori parrish, Duy Doan, and Holly Wren Spaulding for your feedback on earlier drafts of the manuscript; Tiana Nobile and all the writers in the revision group who provided valuable feedback on key poems; and to Faith Adiele, Serena W. Lin, and the whole BIPOC Writing Community for hilarity, connection, and inspiration during the pandemic. Particular thanks to members of the Catalyst Circle for helping me turn my dream into reality: Ching-In Chen, cori parrish, Franny Choi, Jane Park, Michél Legendre, Sarah Gambito, and Sarah Hodgdon.

And most of all, with so much gratitude and vast love for Patti and the beautiful we build.

RECENT TITLES FROM ALICE JAMES BOOKS

If This Is the Age We End Discovery, Rosebud Ben-Oni
Pretty Tripwire, Alessandra Lynch
Inheritance, Taylor Johnson
The Voice of Sheila Chandra, Kazim Ali
Arrow, Sumita Chakraborty
Country, Living, Ira Sadoff
Hot with the Bad Things, Lucia LoTempio
Witch, Philip Matthews
Neck of the Woods, Amy Woolard
Little Envelope of Earth Conditions, Cori A. Winrock
Aviva-No, Shimon Adaf, Translated by Yael Segalovitz
Half/Life: New & Selected Poems, Jeffrey Thomson
Odes to Lithium, Shira Erlichman
Here All Night, Jill McDonough
To the Wren: Collected & New Poems, Jane Mead
Angel Bones, Ilyse Kusnetz
Monsters I Have Been, Kenji C. Liu
Soft Science, Franny Choi
Bicycle in a Ransacked City: An Elegy, Andrés Cerpa
Anaphora, Kevin Goodan
Ghost, like a Place, Iain Haley Pollock
Isako Isako, Mia Ayumi Malhotra
Of Marriage, Nicole Cooley
The English Boat, Donald Revell
We, the Almighty Fires, Anna Rose Welch
DiVida, Monica A. Hand
pray me stay eager, Ellen Doré Watson
Some Say the Lark, Jennifer Chang
Calling a Wolf a Wolf, Kaveh Akbar

Alice James Books is committed to publishing books that matter. The press was founded in 1973 in Boston, Massachusetts as a cooperative, wherein authors performed the day-to-day undertakings of the press. This element remains present today, as authors who publish with the press are invited to collaborate closely in the publication process of their work. AJB remains committed to its founders' original feminist mission, while expanding upon the scope to include all voices and poets who might otherwise go unheard. In keeping with its efforts to build equity and increase inclusivity in publishing and the literary arts, AJB seeks out poets whose writing possesses the range, depth, and ability to cultivate empathy in our world and to dynamically push against silence. The press was named for Alice James, sister to William and Henry, whose extraordinary gift for writing went unrecognized during her lifetime.

Designed by Tiani Kennedy

Printed by McNaughton & Gunn

CPSIA information can be obtained
at www.ICGtesting.com
Printed in the USA
JSHW060923080722
27674JS00003B/9